"I wish I could hold your hand..."

a child's guide to grief and loss

Dr. Pat Palmer
Author of *Liking Myself* and *The Mouse, The Monster and Me*
illustrated by Dianne O'Quinn Burke

Little Imp Books

Impact & Publishers®
ATASCADERO, CALIFORNIA 93423

BAYVILLE FREE LIBRARY

Copyright © 1994, 2000
by Pat Palmer
Eighth Printing, August 2009

All rights reserved under International and Pan-American Copyright Conventions. No part of this book may be reproduced, stored in a retrieval system, or transmitted in any form or by any means, electronic, mechanical, photocopying, recording or otherwise, without express written permission of the author or publisher, except for brief quotations in critical reviews.

Impact Publishers and colophon are registered trademarks of Impact Publishers, Inc.

Library of Congress Cataloging-in-Publication Data

Palmer, Pat, 1928-
    "I wish I could hold your hand-" : a child's guide to grief and loss / by Pat Palmer: illustrated by Dianne O'Quinn Burke.
        p.   cm.
    ISBN 0-915166-82-8
    1. Grief-Juvenile literature.   2. Loss (Psychology) - Juvenile literature.
  3. Bereavement - Psychological aspects - Juvenile literature.   4. Death - Psychological aspects - Juvenile literature.   I. Burke, Dianne O'Quinn.
BF575.G7P35   1994
155.9'37-dc20
                                                                             94-25611
                                                                                  CIP
                                                                                   AC

Printed in the United States of America on acid-free, recycled paper.

Published by
Impact Publishers®
POST OFFICE BOX 6016
ATASCADERO, CALIFORNIA 93423-6016
www.impactpublishers.com

This book is dedicated to all the people who believe it is brave and grown up to hold in their feelings when they have lost a loved one. It is written for all the heartaches never spoken and the oceans of tears that have never been shed.
— Pat Palmer

In sweet rememberance of Violet, who touched us all with her humor and gentle spirit, My Mother, who through her infinite love and solicitude lives forever through me, her grandchildren and great-grandchildren. Her unconditional love continues to guide and embrace us for all time.
— Dianne O'Quinn Burke

It feels good to have someone to love.

That someone can be...
 a mom, or a dad...
 or a teddy bear, or a pet...

Sometimes we have lots of people
 or pets
 to love.

And sometimes the people or pets
  we love
    have to leave...

People go away because they get a divorce...
   or get a job far away...
   or go to jail...
   or join the circus...

Maybe your best friend had to move away
   with her family...
   or your brother went away to college...
   or you had to give away your cat
   because your sister was allergic...

People and pets go away for a
   lot of different reasons.

And sometimes people die.

Sometimes pets die, too.

Everything that is living will die some day,
  even plants and insects.

But when someone you love dies, it doesn't feel good.

It hurts.

When a person or a pet goes away and leaves you
   it doesn't mean he or she stops loving you,
   or caring for you,
   or thinking about you.

The loved one just isn't around
 so you can say:

 "I miss you."
 "I love you."
 "I want to hug you."
 "I wish I could hold your hand."

Sometimes it feels as if your loved one
 is still somewhere nearby,

You can imagine he or she is around,
 still loving you.
You can feel the love.

You can imagine your loved one
 is with you as you read this.

It's not your fault when someone goes away.

People have their own reasons for leaving.

<u>You</u> don't make others go away.

When people or pets you love leave,
   it's normal to feel sad, lonely, scared,
      and even guilty or angry because they left.
Lots of people have these feelings.

Even though feelings hurt,
   it's better to feel them
   than to push them away,
   or down,
   or to try to hide them.

Even if you try <u>not</u> to feel the feelings
   you still have them somewhere inside you.

These feelings stay with you
   year after year.
You may feel a little bit upset
   all the time.

Sometimes the feelings that stay in your body
   can cause aches and pains,
   or sickness...

or just a sad expression on your face.

Even though it hurts to feel the pain
 of losing someone you love,
  it's important to feel it now.

If you don't,
 the feelings can stay tucked away
 for a long, long time.

When someone you love leaves
   it's better to feel the sadness
   and to learn to deal with your feelings...
   than to carry them with you forever!

When someone you love leaves...
   it's O.K. to let the hurt in your heart show.

You can show you're hurting in different ways...

A lot of people cry.

Sometimes they get grumpy,
   or sad, or quiet...

You can cry if you want to...

It's O.K. to cry.
It can help you feel better.

People understand when you cry.
Sometimes they will cry with you.

Crying is a good way to show how you feel.

Let your tears flow.

Your tears are beautiful and healing.

Tears help you
 to feel all of your sadness.

Tears are like raindrops in your heart,
 washing away the hurt and pain
 of your loss.

When someone you love leaves, it's a good time to cry.

Sometimes it's very hard to believe that someone you love
    is really gone.
And sometimes you just can't cry, even if you really want to.

That's O.K., too. But don't pretend nothing happened...
That won't help you feel better.

And don't worry if you do feel better sometimes.
It's o.k. to laugh and smile and feel happy, too.
You don't have to feel sad all the time.

Sometimes it helps to talk to someone.

It's good to talk about your sadness,
  or your anger, or whatever feelings you have.

You can tell a friend,
  Mother or Father,
  an aunt or uncle,
  a neighbor,
  a teacher, or
  a counselor at school.

Or anyone else you
  really trust.

Talking helps to get the feelings
   up and out
   of your body.

When you talk about your feelings,
   you might feel as if
   you're setting them free.

Sometimes it helps to write a letter to the person or pet
  that left you, even if he or she isn't alive anymore,
  or can't write back to you.
Or you could draw a picture...

Write or draw and tell your loved one what you remember
  about him or her.
Tell how you feel about being left behind.
Write or draw about everything you're feeling.
Tell about what you used to do.
Tell about what he or she is missing now.
Tell about how much you miss him or her.

Be sure to remember the good things,
  and the happy times you had.

You don't have to mail the letter or picture...
  just drawing or writing things down can be good for you.

When someone you love leaves it is a time to be especially good to yourself.

When you feel scared, sad, or lonely,
   go sit with a friend or a pet.

Ask for hugs.

Snuggle with your parent,
   and ask him or her to rock you.

Or cuddle a teddy bear,
   and rock yourself.

Take care of that tender part inside you
    where it hurts the most.

When you feel lost and alone,
   ask yourself:

   What do I really want
   and need right now?

   How can I help myself
   feel better?

   How can other people help me
   feel better?

   Who can I ask to help me now?

Remember...

   it is a good thing to let yourself feel
   the empty space in your life
   from losing someone you love.

And know that

   Love never really goes away.

It stays with you

   forever!

More Books With IMPACT

Teen Esteem
A Self-Direction Manual for Young Adults (Third Edition)
Pat Palmer, Ed.D. and Melissa Alberti Froehner
Softcover: $11.95   128 pages   ISBN: 978-1-886230-87-3

Without lecturing or patronizing, helps teenagers develop the skills to handle stress, peer pressure, substance abuse, anger, sexual expression, and more. Includes new material on being different, cyber-bullying, and coping with depression.

Cool Cats, Calm Kids
Relaxation and Stress Management for Young People
Mary Williams, M.A.
Softcover: $8.95   32 pages   ISBN: 978-0-915166-94-7

Guide to stress management for children 7-12. Uses "cats" as teachers, illustrating catnaps, stretching, "hanging in there." Includes section for parents, teachers, and counselors.

The Divorce Helpbook for Kids
Cynthia MacGregor
Softcover: $13.95   144 pages   ISBN: 978-1-886230-39-2

Down-to-earth guide that helps kids get through the divorce of parents. Topics include the reasons for divorce; ways divorce will change their lives; kids' feelings about divorce; things kids can do to feel better; who to talk to, and what's likely to happen next. Covers life after divorce; visitation, custody, straddling two households.

Also by Cynthia MacGregor: **The Divorce Helpbook for Teens**
Softcover: $13.95   144 pages   ISBN: 978-1-886230-57-6

Impact Publishers®
POST OFFICE BOX 6016 • ATASCADERO, CALIFORNIA 93423-6016
Ask your local or online bookseller, or call 1-800-246-7228 to order direct.
Prices effective August 2009, and subject to change without notice.
Free catalog of self-help and professional resources: visit www.impactpublishers.com

---

Since 1970 — Psychology you can use, from professionals you can trust.